Declare the
Word of God
Over Your Life

Prayer Journal

Nyiesha Harrington

FINA PRESS™

FINA PRESS™

GOD OF THE IMPOSSIBLE

"For with God nothing shall be impossible."

LUKE 1:37, KJV

Dedication

I would like to dedicate this journal and devotional to my beautiful children Torrell and Ta'Nyiah Golson, who are my precious gems. They were born at the time when God called me to start my faith journey with Him. I knew when they where babies that my life would never be the same. God used them to bring structure and unconditional love to my life in a way that I didn't know I needed. They have been the fruit and evidence of God's grace and mercy to me. As I offered my body a living sacrifice to Jesus I watched as it yielded to Him, and how my obedience to Him continues to break generation curses and establishes generational blessings in our family. Thank you Lord, for giving me your heart in these two beautiful young adults. I love you both more than you could ever know.

Table of Contents

Introduction

Let me declare right now that your life will never be the same again. By faith I believe that for every person reading this journal, things are turning around for your good. Do you believe it? I know it can be difficult to believe when the pieces of your life seem scattered, or your prayers seem to be hitting brass, but can I tell you that what seems to be working against you is working together for your good. You may not see how the broken pieces of your life can possibly come together but can I remind you that if you are still breathing God is still working and what He has for you is far greater than what's behind you.

Miracles happen every day. I personally can testify about how many times God brought me out of difficulties and through them, but He is not finished with me yet, and He is not finished with you either. He is still working to bring to past the very plans that He predestined to come to past in our lives according to Jeremiah 29:11, "For I know the plans I have for you," declares the Lord, "plans to prosper you and not to harm you, plans to give you hope and a future" (NIV).

He is not just the God of the past, but He is a very present help in the time of trouble (Psalms 46:1). Be encouraged, your season is changing. God can turn your morning to dancing (Psalms 30 11-12) and your sorrows to joy (John 16:20).

Psalms 77:14-15 reminds us "You are the God who performs miracles; you display your power among the peoples. With your mighty arm you redeemed your people, the descendants of Jacob and Joseph" (NIV). God is still performing miracles and redeeming His people every day. You will testify.

God wants to display His power in your life today. Join me in activating the promises of God over our lives. This next season is "Voice-activated" and this is going to require our participation. Like you, I am waiting for specific prayer request to be answered, and by faith I am confident that our Father will show up "on time."

This journal is designed to help you be specific and strategic in your prayers, in declaring God's word over your life, your marriage, children, health, area of influence, and standing when you don't see any movement. We are not moved by what we see but what we know; and we know our God is a promise keeper, a miracle worker, light in the darkness, and faithful to perfect everything concerning us.

How to Pray

In the Blue Letter Bible (2023), Don Steward defines *prayer* as talking to God. He states that it is our way of communication our thoughts, needs, and desires to Him. In other words, prayer is an act, not merely an attitude.

Many people have a hard time praying. The question is: Why? We can certainly come up with many reasons why, but I speculate from many years of being a leader in ministry that many people are not sure how to talk to God. Prayer is not supposed to be difficult but simple and way to build relationship with the Father.

Jesus said in Matthew 6: 5-15 MSG

Pray with Simplicity

"And when you come before God, don't turn that into a theatrical production either. All these people making a regular show out of their prayers, hoping for fifteen minutes of fame! Do you think God sits in a box seat?

"Here's what I want you to do: Find a quiet, secluded place so you won't be tempted to role-play before God. Just be there as simply and honestly as you can manage. The focus will shift from you to God, and you will begin to sense his grace.

"The world is full of so-called prayer warriors who are prayer-ignorant. They're full of formulas and programs and advice, peddling techniques for getting what you want from God. Don't fall for that nonsense. This is your Father you are dealing with, and he knows yo ur needs, better than you do. With a God like this loving you, you can pray very simply.

Like this:

Our Father in heaven,
Reveal who you are.
Set the world right;
Do what's best—
as above, so below.
Keep us alive with three square meals.
Keep us forgiven with you and forgiving others.
Keep us safe from ourselves and the devil.
You're in charge!
You can do anything you want!
You're ablaze in beauty!
Yes. Yes. Yes.

"In prayer there is a connection between what God does and what you do. You can't get forgiveness from God, for instance, without also forgiving others. If you refuse to do your part, you cut yourself off from God's part."

Praying the Word

Praying the word of God is an important strategy to see God's word come to pass in your life. Remember we discuss earlier Jeremiah 29:11 where it says: "For I know the plans I have for you," declares the Lord, "plans to prosper you and not to harm you, plans to give you hope and a future.

If God knows the plans, the question should be what are those plans. The apostle Paul prays in Ephesians 1:16-19 that the God of our Lord Jesus Christ, the Father of glory, may give unto you the spirit of wisdom and revelation in the knowledge of him; and that The eyes of your understanding being enlightened; that ye may know what is the hope of his calling, and what the riches of the glory of his inheritance in the saints, And what is the exceeding greatness of his power to us who believe, according to the working of his mighty power" (KJV).

What is the apostle Paul saying in those verses? He is saying that there are things that God has given us that remain hidden, and we need the Spirit of God to reveal to us what they are, and not just the things but also to know who Him better.

It is difficult to talk to someone when you don't have a relationship with them and even if you know of them when you have a need mostly likely you won't ask. Why? Because relationship is the key.

When you are confident in your relationship with someone you no longer ask with uncertainty or doubt but faith and belief. You know by working with them what they can or cannot do. God, however, is not limited like man, but His word suggest that there is away to come to him. He has already helped us to understand that through His word we can be specific in our communication with Him because has already us certain things.

Let's Pray

Spirit of the living God, fall fresh over each person, married couple, family, church, nation, and heart reading this prayer. May they each have a divine encounter with you. Father, I thank you for those who have committed to redicating their life back to you; in relationship, prayer, word, and call.

We repent for trying to do things in our own strength. We desperately need you. Purify us, cleanse, heal us, and revive us. You said in your word: "if my people, who are called by my name, will humble themselves and pray, and seek my face and turn from their wicked ways, then I will hear from heaven, and I will forgive their sin and will heal their land" (2 Chronicles 7:14).

Today we offer our bodies a living sacrifice, holy, acceptable to God, which is our reasonable service (Romans 12:1). Father, let a hunger and thirst be our portion in this season and for the rest of our lives. Lord light a fire in our hearts, and may our light never go dim. May we be a people who are prepared and ready to serve, love, and lead others to your saving grace.

Lord, we come boldly to the throne of grace that we may obtain mercy and find grace to help in time of need. Give us the grace to make changes, the grace to start over, the grace to believe again, the grace to hope again, the grace to pray again, the grace to spend time in your presence, the grace to seek you with our whole hearts.

Thank you, Lord, that with you nothing is impossible. You are able to do exceedingly abundantly above all that we ask or think, according to the power that worketh in us. Let your resurrecting power move in the lives of your people today. I prophesy that every dry in their lives must live, and anything that died prematurely let you your breath cause it to come back to like again.

Father, I, Nyiesha Harrington, stand in the gap and pray over your people today. May every breach be closed. May every home be restored, may chains be broken. May the grace of the Lord Jesus Christ, the love of God, and the communion of the Holy Ghost, be with you all. Amen.

Now unto him that is able to keep you from falling, and to present you faultless before the presence of his glory with exceeding joy, To the only wise God our Savior, be glory and majesty, dominion and power, both now and ever. Amen.

Chapter 1

Declaring God's Word Over Your Life

"I AM WHO GOD SAYS I AM"

*"Therefore, if anyone is in Christ, he is a new creation;
old things have passed away; behold, all things have become new."*

2 Corinthians 5:17, NKJV

"Before I formed you in the womb I knew you; Before you were born I sanctified you; I ordained you a prophet to the nations."

Jeremiah 1:7, NKJV

-NSH

"I will praise You, for I am fearfully and wonderfully made;
Marvelous are Your works, And that my soul knows very well."

Psalms 139:14, NKJV

"For you are all sons of God through faith in Christ Jesus.
For as many of you as were baptized into Christ have put on Christ.
There is neither Jew nor Greek, there is neither slave nor free,
there is neither male nor female; for you are all one in Christ Jesus."

Galatians 3:26-28, NKJV

-NSH

*"But you are a chosen race, a royal priesthood, a holy nation,
a people for his own possession, that you may proclaim the excellencies
of him who called you out of darkness into his marvelous light."*

1 Peter 2:9

-NSH

"I have been crucified with Christ. It is no longer I who live, but Christ who lives in me. And the life I now live in the flesh I live by faith in the Son of God, who loved me and gave himself for me."

Galatians 2:20

-NSH

Chapter 2

Declaring God's Will Over Your Life

"GOD HAS GOOD PLANS FOR ME"

"'For I know the plans I have for you,' declares the LORD,
'plans to prosper you and not to harm you,
plans to give you hope and a future.'"

Jeremiah 29:11, NIV

*"And who knows whether you have not come
to the kingdom for such a time as this?"*

Esther 4:14

-NSH

"And we know that for those who love God all things work together for good, for those who are called according to his purpose."

Romans 8:28

-NSH

"This is good, and pleases God our Savior, who wants all people to be saved and to come to a knowledge of the truth."

1 Timothy 2:3-4

_____

_____

_____

_____

_____

_____

_____

_____

_____

_____

_____

_____

_____

_____

_____

_____

_____

_____

-NSH

"Give thanks in all circumstances;
for this is the will of God in Christ Jesus for you."

1 Thessalonians 5:18

_____

_____

_____

_____

_____

_____

_____

_____

_____

_____

_____

_____

_____

_____

_____

_____

_____

_____

-NSH

"Now may the God of peace, who through the blood of the eternal covenant brought back from the dead our Lord Jesus, that great Shepherd of the sheep, equip you with everything good for doing his will, and may he work in us what is pleasing to him, through Jesus Christ, to whom be glory for ever and ever. Amen."

Hebrews 13:20-21, NIV

-NSH

Chapter 3

Declaring God's Word Over Your Marriage

"THE SACREDNESS OF MARRIAGE"

"Then the Lord God said, "It is not good that the man should be alone; I will make him a helper fit for him."

Genesis 2:18

"He who finds a wife finds a good thing and obtains favor from the Lord."

Proverbs 18:22

-NSH

"Therefore a man shall leave his father and his mother and hold fast to his wife, and they shall become one flesh."

Genesis 2:24

-NSH

"Love is patient and kind; love does not envy or boast; it is not arrogant or rude. It does not insist on its own way; it is not irritable or resentful; it does not rejoice at wrongdoing, but rejoices with the truth. Love bears all things, believes all things, hopes all things, endures all things."

1 Corinthians 13:4-7

-NSH

"Wives, submit to your husbands, as is fitting in the Lord. Husbands, love your wives, and do not be harsh with them."

Colossians 3:18-19

"Let marriage be held in honor among all, and let the marriage bed be undefiled, for God will judge the sexually immoral and adulterous."

Hebrews 13:4

Chapter 4

Declaring God's Word Over Your Children

"THE CALL OF A PARENT"

*"Train up a child in the way he should go
and even when he is old, he will not depart from it."*

Proverbs 22:6

"But the mercy of the Lord is from everlasting to everlasting on those who fear Him, and His righteousness to children's children."

Psalms 103:17

"When Jesus saw this, he was indignant. He said to them, 'Let the little children come to me, and do not hinder them, for the kingdom of God belongs to such as these.'"

Mark 10:14, NIV

-NSH

"May he give you the desire of your heart and make all your plans succeed. May we shout for joy over your victory and lift up our banners in the name of our God. May the Lord grant all your requests."

Psalms 20:4-5

-NSH

"I remain confident of this: I will see the goodness of the Lord in the land of the living. Wait for the Lord; be strong and take heart and wait for the Lord."

Psalms 27:13-14

-NSH

Chapter 5

Declaring God's Word Over Your Health

"BE HEALED"

"But he was pierced for our transgressions; he was crushed for our iniquities; upon him was the chastisement that brought us peace, and with his wounds we are healed."

Isaiah 53:5

"Behold, I will bring to it health and healing, and I will heal them and reveal to them abundance of prosperity and security."

Jeremiah 33:6

"And the prayer of faith will save the one who is sick, and the Lord will raise him up. And if he has committed sins, he will be forgiven."

James 5:15

-NSH

"For I will restore health to you, and your wounds I will heal, declares the Lord, because they have called you an outcast: 'It is Zion, for whom no one cares!'"

Jeremiah 30:17

-NSH

"He heals the brokenhearted and binds up their wounds."

Psalms 147:3

"A joyful heart is good medicine, but a crushed spirit dries up the bones."

Proverbs 17:22

-NSH

Chapter 6

Declaring God's Word
Over Your Land

"RESTORATION"

*"If my people who are called by my name humble themselves,
and pray and seek my face and turn from their wicked ways, then
I will hear from heaven and will forgive their sin and heal their land."*

2 Chronicles 7:14

"And I will bless them that bless thee, and curse him that curseth thee: and in thee shall all families of the earth be blessed."

Genesis 12:3, KJV

-NSH

"Pray for the peace of Jerusalem: they shall prosper that love thee."

Psalms 122:6, KJV

-NSH

"If my people, who are called by my name, will humble themselves and pray and seek my face and turn from their wicked ways, then I will hear from heaven, and I will forgive their sin and will heal their land."

2 Chronicles 7:14, NIV

-NSH

Chapter 7

Standing on God's Word

"I AM STANDING MY GROUND"

"Finally, be strong in the Lord and in the strength of his might.
Put on the whole armor of God, that you may be able to stand against
the schemes of the devil. For we do not wrestle against flesh and blood,
but against the rulers, against the authorities, against the cosmic powers over
this present darkness, against the spiritual forces of evil in the heavenly places.
Therefore take up the whole armor of God, that you may be able to withstand
in the evil day, and having done all, to stand firm. Stand therefore, having
fastened on the belt of truth, and having put on the breastplate of righteousness."

Ephesians 6:10-14

"That the God of our Lord Jesus Christ, the Father of glory, may give you the Spirit of wisdom and of revelation in the knowledge of him, having the eyes of your hearts enlightened, that you may know what is the hope to which he has called you, what are the riches of his glorious inheritance in the saints."

Ephesians 1:17-18

-NSH

"In that day you will ask nothing of me. Truly, truly, I say to you, whatever you ask of the Father in my name, he will give it to you. Until now you have asked nothing in my name. Ask, and you will receive, that your joy may be full."

John 16:23-24

-NSH

"If you abide in me, and my words abide in you, ask whatever you wish, and it will be done for you. By this my Father is glorified, that you bear much fruit and so prove to be my disciples."

John 15:7-8

-NSH

"Truly, I say to you, whatever you bind on earth shall be bound in heaven, and whatever you loose on earth shall be loosed in heaven. Again I say to you, if two of you agree on earth about anything they ask, it will be done for them by my Father in heaven. For where two or three are gathered in my name, there am I among them."

Matthew 18:18-20

_____

_____

_____

_____

_____

_____

_____

_____

_____

_____

_____

_____

_____

_____

_____

_____

_____

_____

_____

-NSH

*"Let us then with confidence draw near to the throne of grace,
that we may receive mercy and find grace to help in time of need."*

Hebrews 4:16

-NSH

Always Pray

"Have faith in God," Jesus answered. "Truly I tell you, if anyone says to this mountain, 'Go, throw yourself into the sea,' and does not doubt in their heart but believes that what they say will happen, it will be done for them. Therefore I tell you, whatever you ask for in prayer, believe that you have received it, and it will be yours. And when you stand praying, if you hold anything against anyone, forgive them, so that your Father in heaven may forgive you your sins."

Mark 11:22-25, NIV

Printed in the USA
CPSIA information can be obtained
at www.ICGtesting.com
LVHW071115221223
767112LV00085B/3570